Fish Do WHAT? In the Water

The Secret Lives of Marine Animals

by Caroline Patterson

illustrations by Robert Rath

FARCOUNTRY PRESS

Helena, Montana

Dedicated to Tobin, Fish Lover of Fifth Street

Acknowledgments

I wish to acknowledge an enormous debt of gratitude to Lisa Eby, associate professor of fish biology at the University of Montana, for her expertise and enthusiasm in working on this book. I also wish to thank Tim Carpenter of the Seattle Aquarium for his help with the Pacific red octopus.

A heartfelt thank you to friend and illustrator Robert Rath for his inspired artwork, and Tom Stack for his remarkable and beautiful photography. Finally, thanks to my friends at Farcountry Press, particularly Sue Johnson, whose title inspired this book; Linda Netschert and Kathy Springmeyer, who brought it into being; Jessica Solberg, the soul of patience and an excellent editor; Andrea Rud, for her sharp editorial eye; and Shirley Machonis, for her artistic flair.

ISBN 10: 1-56037-519-1
ISBN 13: 978-1-56037-519-7

For more information on our books, write Farcountry Press, P.O. Box 5630, Helena, MT 59604; call (800) 821-3874; or visit www.farcountrypress.com.

Library of Congress Cataloging-in-Publication Data

Patterson, Caroline, 1956-
Fish do what in the water? / by Caroline Patterson.
p. cm.
ISBN 978-1-56037-519-7
1. Marine fishes--Juvenile literature. 2. Marine animals--Juvenile literature. I. Title.
QL620.P386 2012
597.177--dc23

2012003152

Created, produced, and designed in the United States.
Manufactured by Everbest Printing
334 Huanshi Road South
Dachong Western Industrial District
Panyu, Guangdong, China
January 2012
Printed in China.

16 15 14 13 12 1 2 3 4 5

Table of Contents

Fish Do What in the Water?

A Fish Is a Fish Is a Fish . . . Sort Of

IF I ASKED YOU TO DRAW A STICK FIGURE of a fish, you might make a loop for the head and body, a triangle for the tail, a few sideways Vs for fins, and a couple of slashes for gills. Presto! A fish. But that basic stick figure is just the beginning. There are nearly 30,000 species of fish—big fish, little fish, fish that change colors to match their surroundings, fish with poisonous fins or lights over their heads, and even fish that suck the guts out of other fish.

parrotfish
dorsal fin
caudal fin
anal fin
pectoral fin
pelvic fin
clownfish
eggs

What a Fish Is

So what is a fish? Fish are animals that are **vertebrates** *(VER-tuh-brets)*, which is a fancy way to say they have a backbone. They are cold-blooded and live in the water. Usually fish lay eggs and have scales, fins, tails, and gills.

humpback whale

What a Fish Isn't

Now let's get something straight. Some of the creatures in this book are not fish. **Dolphins, porpoises,** and **whales** are **mammals.** Why? Because they are warm-blooded—which means their inside body temperature stays the same no matter what the temperature is outside—and they depend upon their mother's milk when they are babies. They also have hair. Baby whales and dolphins are even born with moustaches!

sea nettle jelly

sea stars

And don't call **jellyfish** or **starfish** "fish" either, even though "fish" is part of their name. They are **invertebrates** *(in-VER-tuh-brets)*, or creatures without backbones. These include the ghostly looking jellies. Many jellies look like open parachutes as they move through the water. They include **bloody-belly comb jellies, blue jellies,** and **sea nettle jellies.** Prickly **sea cucumber,** spiderlike **apple anemones,** and **sea stars** don't have backbones either.

Atlantic bottlenose dolphin

Largest Mammal

The world's **largest mammal** is the **blue whale.** It weighs 150 tons—as much as **a train engine.** Its **tongue** alone weighs as much as **two Volkswagen Beetles**—about two tons.

The **squid, cuttlefish,** and **octopus** are **cephalopods** *(SEHF-uh-lo-pods),* which is Greek for "head-feet." It makes sense, when you think about it. That's what these sea animals look like—all head and feet.

giant cuttlefish

giant Pacific octopus

And don't forget the animals with soft bodies that carry their homes around with them: **lobsters, crayfish,** and **crabs.** They are called **crustaceans** *(crus-TAY-shunz).* They don't have backbones or fins, but watch out for those claws!

northern lobster in eel grass

Cold-Blooded

Fish are **cold-blooded.** That doesn't mean they aren't nice. It means they are **ectotherms** *(ECK-toh-thermz)*. The temperature of an ectotherm's body matches the temperature of its surroundings: cold water, cold body; warm water, warm body.

whale shark

The **largest fish** is the **whale shark,** which can grow to be fifty-nine feet long. That's still about twenty feet shorter than the blue whale. The **smallest fish** is one you could barely see in your hand. It is the female ***Paedocypris*** *(pay-doh-SIP-ris)*, a tiny half-inch-long fish that belongs to the carp family. See-through, with large eyes and unusual fins, it was discovered in 2006.

Jaws

Sharks are known for their teeth-filled jaws. But some fish have no jaws at all. The ancient **lamprey** species is one example of a jawless fish. Even though today's lamprey looks a lot different from its great-great-great-great-grandparent lamprey, it shares traits like jawless mouths, rudimentary backbones, and tail fins. Another jawless fish is the **hagfish.** It looks like a worm, creates stinky slime, and ties itself up in the most amazing shapes.

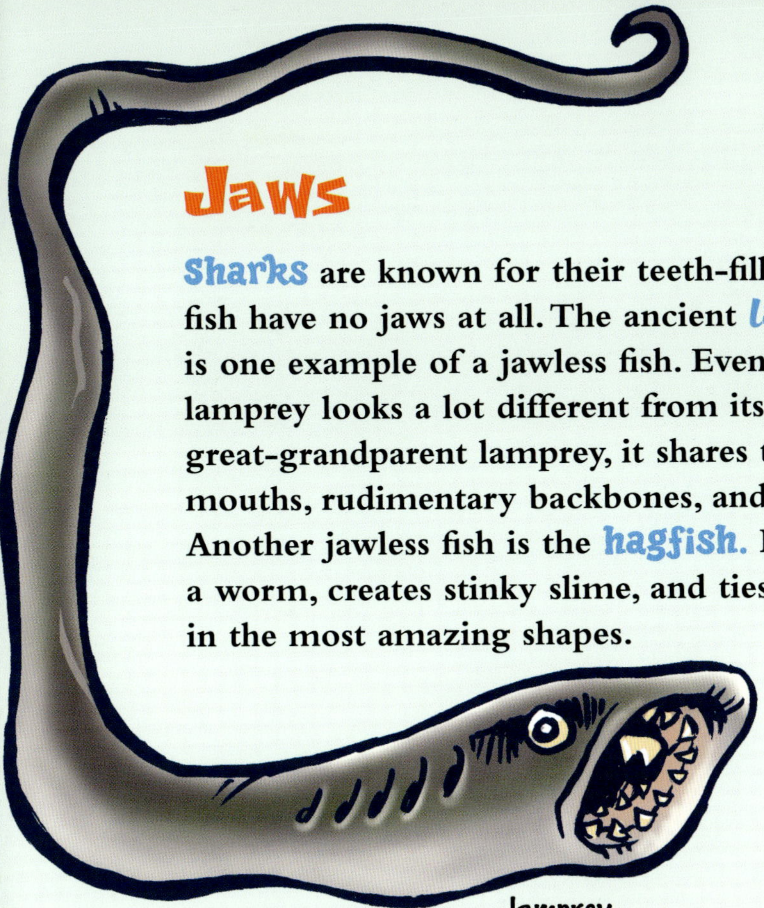

The World's Oceans

Although several of the fish in this book live in rivers or lakes, most of the creatures we've described, indeed most of the world's fish, live in the ocean.

Ocean Depths

Vast and mysterious, the ocean has undersea mountain ranges, canyons, vents, and regions so deep they remain permanently in the dark. Most of the world's marine animals live in five zones that are based on the amount of light they receive: the **Sunlight Zone,** the **Twilight Zone,** the **Midnight Zone,** the **Abyss,** and the **Trenches.**

The Sunlight Zone: Although this is the smallest of the five ocean zones, about 90 percent of all marine life lives here. The sunlight in this zone makes **photosynthesis** *(fo-toh-SIN-the-sis)* possible. This is the process by which sunlight and carbon dioxide gas are converted into fuel for plants to grow.

0 to 656 feet (0 to 200 meters)

The Twilight Zone: The top part of this zone receives faint or filtered sunlight during the day, but the lower part is always dark. No plants grow here.

656 to 3,281 feet (200 to 1,000 meters)

The Midnight Zone: Deep and dark, this area of the ocean doesn't get any sunlight. Some of the animals living here don't even have eyes.

3,281 to 13,123 feet (1,000 to 4,000 meters)

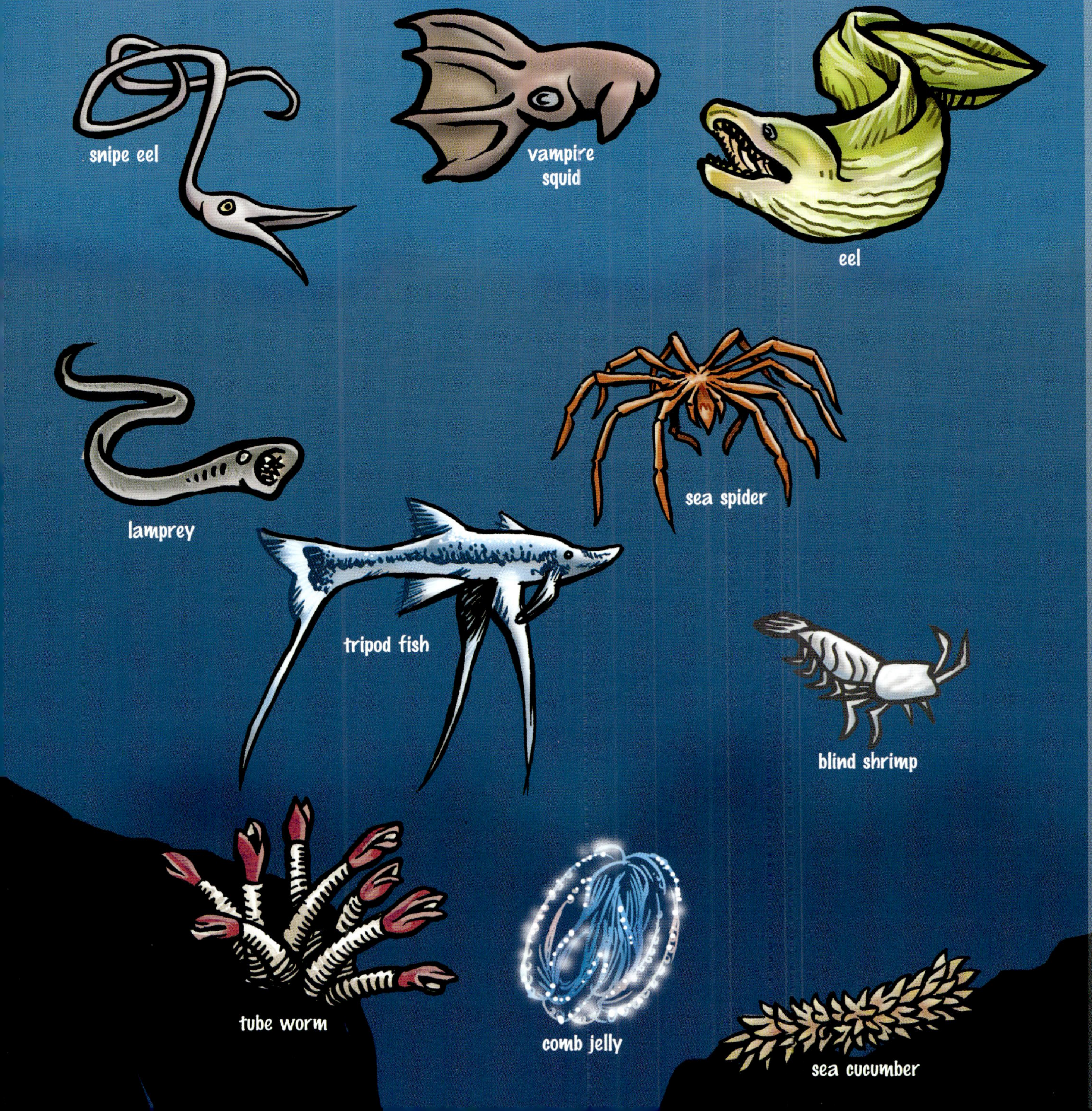

13,123 to 19,685 feet (4,000 to 6,000 meters)

The Abyss:
Derived from the Greek word for "bottomless," this deep-sea area is permanently dark. The abyssal plain makes up 90 percent of the ocean.

19,685 feet (6,000 meters)

The Trenches:
The other name for this zone, the Hadal Zone, comes from the Greek word *Hades,* which means "unseen" or "underworld." This zone is permanently dark, with water temperatures barely above freezing. The deepest point in the ocean is located in the Mariana Trench off the coast of Japan at 35,797 feet (10,911 meters) deep.

In the Beginning

FISH HAVE MANY DIFFERENT WAYS of **meeting, mating,** and **giving birth.** Some have mating rituals, others don't. Some females lay millions of eggs, others just one. Some lay eggs and are done with their young; other fish spend time taking care of their little ones.

pregnant male sea horse

Fish Dates

Sea horses conduct a twirling courtship dance before mating. But instead of the female carrying the babies, the male prepares to do it. The male puffs up his belly, or **brood pouch,** to show he is ready to receive the female's eggs, and the female lays the eggs there. Two to six weeks later, the small sea horses come swimming out. Welcome to the world!

female (left) and male cuttlefish

Male **cuttlefish** fight each other for the coolest pad—or mating den—to attract females. The cuttlefish embrace and mate. After the eggs are fertilized, the female cuttlefish coats them with a protective covering. Then she cements them to the roof of the mating den.

Hiding Eggs

Life at sea can be rough going for fish eggs waiting to hatch, so fish have developed ways to protect them. **Lesser-spotted dogfish** lay eggs with armored cases, known as "mermaid's purses." **Salmon** dig nests in rivers that flow into oceans to lay their eggs. The male and female lie together in the nest, then the female lays the eggs and the male fertilizes them. The female buries the eggs by sweeping gravel over the nest with her tail.

Yellow-headed jawfish and **cichlids** *(SICK-lids)*, on the other hand, have found another safe place to store their eggs until they hatch—in their mouths!

The number of eggs different fish produce varies wildly. The **ocean sunfish** lays as many as 300 million eggs in one spawning. Each year, **barracudas** lay 200,000 eggs; by contrast the **devil ray** produces just one.

Hatched or Born

Most fish are hatched from eggs. Some fish, however, including **sharks, guppies,** and **mollies,** give birth to live young. The **blacktip shark** may carry her young for up to sixteen months before giving birth. That's almost twice the length of a human pregnancy. **Sand tiger sharks** develop in numerous eggs in the mother's two **uteruses** *(YOU-ter-us-ehz),* which are the places inside the mother where the sharks grow until they are born. The largest hatchling in each of the two uteruses, however, eats the other unhatched eggs and smaller embryos. When the female shark gives birth, just two shark babies are born.

Pity the poor **octopus** mom. After she lays her eggs, nearly 50,000 of them, she stays close by, guarding them from predators for nearly forty days. She also blows currents of water on the eggs. Why? To provide them with oxygen. There is only one problem. She doesn't have time to search for her own supper. Yup, mom doesn't eat until the babies are born. Now that's dedication.

Bringing Up Baby

Blue whales, orcas, and **dolphins** are mammals, and the babies drink their mother's milk. A blue whale baby drinks 100 gallons of milk each day! With an appetite like that, the calf grows quickly. At seven months of age, the calf gains an average of nine pounds an hour.

Atlantic bottlenose dolphin

Dolphins stay with their mothers until they are nearly five years old. They learn by copying or "mirroring" their mothers' movements. Mom dives; baby dives. Mom fishes; baby fishes. The moms also teach the young to play with their food—throwing a fish back and forth with the other dolphins—before eating it. Why? Scientists think it encourages group cooperation.

Orca moms discipline their calves by corralling them and tooth-scratching them. This is mom's way of communicating, "Hey, you weren't listening to me!" or "Behave!"

Gender Benders

From boys to girls, girls to boys, several species change sex during their fish lives. Often male-to-female changes occur in species without territories. The bright-orange-and-white fish known as **clownfish** begin their lives as males, but as they grow, they change into females.

clownfish

queen parrotfish

If **Mardi Gras wrasses, parrotfish,** and **California sheepheads** wrote stories about their lives, they might title them: "Started Off a Girl, Ended Up a Boy." **Hamlets** are male and female at the same time—**hermaphrodites** *(her-MAF-fro-dites)*. When they find mates, each fish takes turns acting male and female.

creole wrasse

shy hamlet

Anglerfish are united in an interesting way. The smaller male anglerfish bites the female. Their flesh is glued together forever. When this happens, he provides her with sperm to fertilize the eggs; she provides him with food.

Among **Atlantic salmon,** there are two kinds of male fish. Larger, more aggressive males do the fighting for breeding territories, and smaller males called "jacks" sneak in to join the breeding.

female (left) and male Atlantic salmon

Cool Body Parts

FISH ARE AT HOME AROUND THE WORLD. Why? Because most of the earth—70 percent—is covered with water. Some fish live in streams and ponds, but most fish live in the ocean. They live at various depths, ranging from the sunlit layers where plants grow to the deepest ocean trenches that never see the light of day. Each type of fish has unique body parts that are specially adapted for life at sea, whether in the bright upper regions or in the cold, dark depths. If you could combine these body parts in one creature, what would it look like?

Body Shape

The shape of a fish's **body** tells a lot about its lifestyle: Streamlined bodies are fast-swimming predators. Check out **sailfish** bodies, shaped like jet airplanes. The rounded **spotted ratfish** with its puffy body and tiny side fins is built more for hiding from predators. Large, flat-sided halibut spend time at the ocean bottom.

Tail shape gives us clues about how fast a fish can swim. Fish with half-moon-shaped tails win the speed trials. The **black marlin** has been clocked swimming at 86.7 miles per hour. Wide, even tails, like those on **trout,** help fish dart this way and that to avoid rocks in our fast-moving rivers.

Check out the tiny pectoral fins on the 5,000-pound mola. The mola uses them to move around, much like we use oars on a rowboat.

Different Strokes

Most fish swim from side to side. Some fish, such as **parrotfish,** have stiff bodies and use their fins like oars to move their bodies along. **Rays** propel themselves forward by moving water up and down with their pectoral fins; it's almost like they are flying through the water.

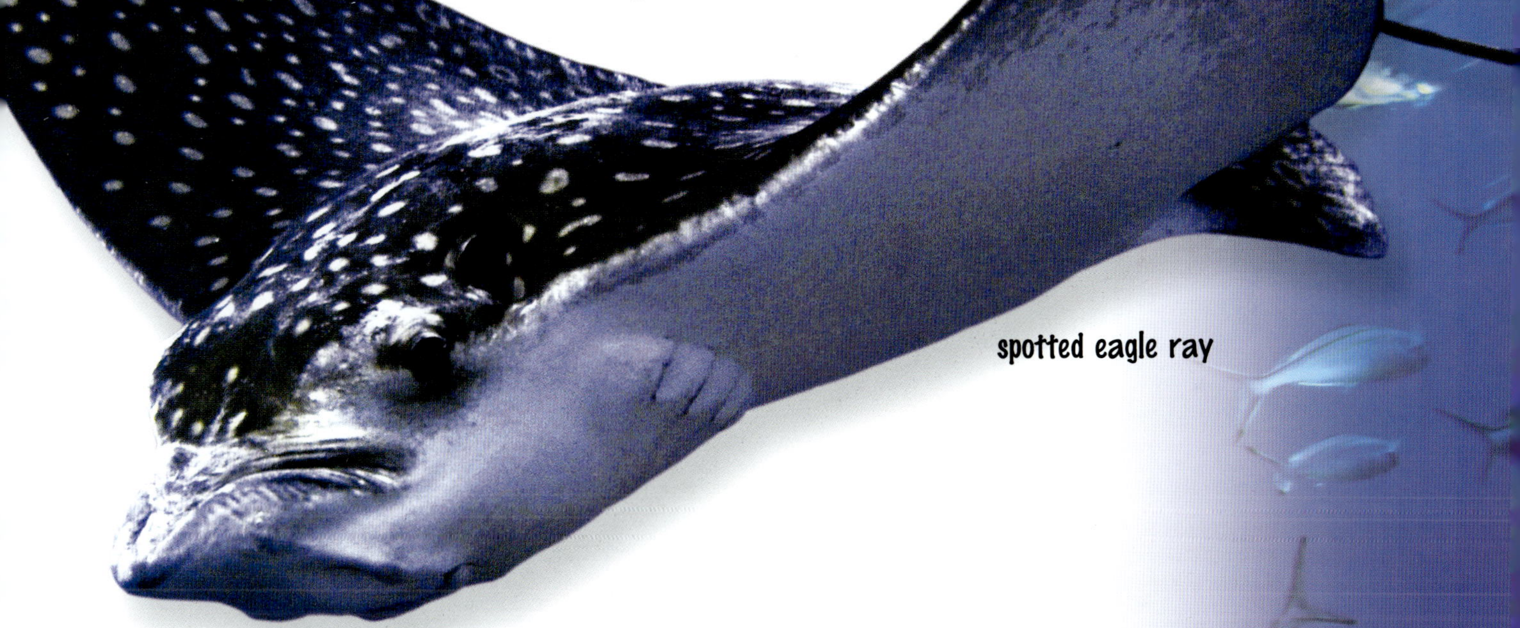

spotted eagle ray

parrotfish

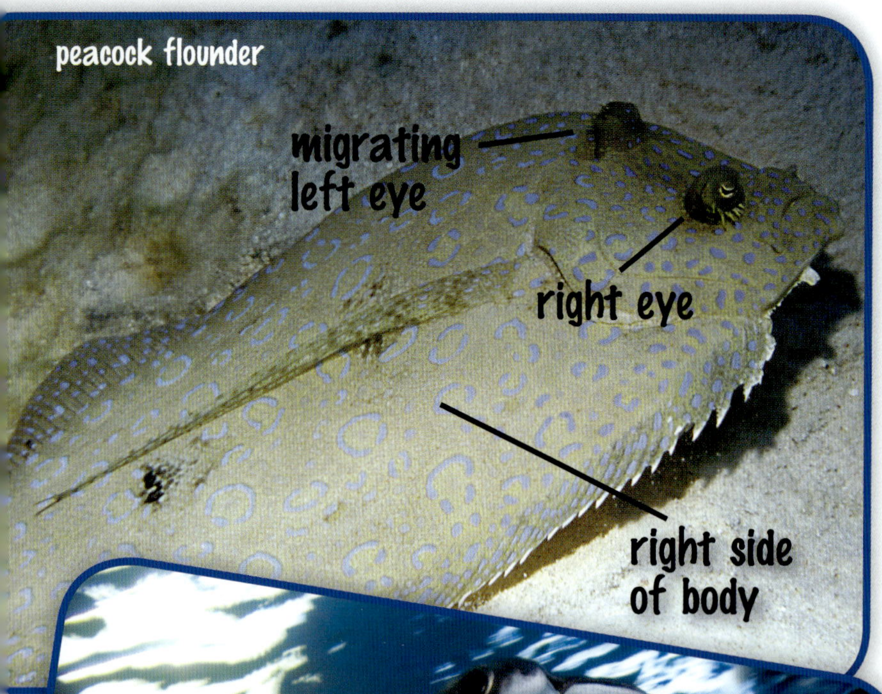

peacock flounder

hammerhead shark

Weird Eyes

All flatfish have two eyes on one side of their heads. At birth, a flatfish (such as a flounder or a halibut) has one eye on each side of its head; but when it is very young, one of its eyes migrates to the other side of its head, joining its other eye. Why? So the fish can lie flat on the ocean floor and still look up.

The eyes of the hammerhead shark look as if they were fixed on the tips of a yardstick that was glued to its face. The hammerhead may look a little weird, but it doesn't have to turn its head to see left or right, which is good because it doesn't have a neck! With these widely spaced eyes, the shark has excellent vision, and it can see both in front and behind itself at all times.

Anableps!

There are even four-eyed fish called anableps! Each eye socket has one eye divided into two parts: one for seeing above the surface of the water and one for seeing below.

From Teeth to Tongues

Say teeth and, of course, the **great white shark** immediately comes to mind. It has 3,000 bread-knife-like, razor-sharp teeth in five to fifteen rows. The first row does most of the grabbing and ripping, and the rest mostly serve as replacement teeth.

Barracudas have fangs to take large, snapping bites of their prey.

Piranhas hunt in groups and can strip a fish to its bones in minutes.

The **hagfish** dines on dead fish and eats them from the inside out. It bites the dead fish and uses its rasping tongue to scoop the fish's insides into its mouth.

Pharyngeal Teeth

Guppies and **suckers** don't appear to have teeth—but watch out! They have teeth in their throat called **pharyngeal** *(far-uhn-JEE-uhl)* **teeth** that operate like molars to crush food before it enters the stomach.

Check out the mouth of the **black drum.** Inside the toothless, fleshy mouth, deep inside the throat, their pharyngeal teeth look like cobblestones. They use them to crush mollusks and shellfish.

humpback whale showing baleen

No Teeth? No Worries!

Whales, some of the largest mammals in the ocean, have no teeth at all. They have **baleen** instead. Baleen is a thick, fibrous substance, something like a toenail. **Baleen whales** use it as a filter in their mouths to strain food, such as krill (a type of shrimp), from ocean water. **Humpback, finback,** and **blue whales** are all baleen whales.

Fish Mouths, Fish Food

Fish mouths are designed to accommodate the fish diet. Take the strong front teeth of the **wolf eel.** They are made for crushing the shells of the crabs, mussels, and snails it feeds on. The thin, pipelike mouth of the **butterfly fish** is perfectly adapted for getting food from rock crevices. And those **parrotfish** with the fused front teeth? They use them to bite off chunks of coral.

Ever notice those whiskers on **catfish?** They are called **barbels** *(BAR-buhlz)* and serve as taste buds. **Carp, goatfish, sturgeon,** and **zebrafish** have barbels, too. They use them to find food in murky water.

Fish Skin

butterfly fish

Most fish are covered with **scales.** These overlapping structures protect the fish's body, just as shingles protect our homes. Bony fishes often have skin that covers their scales. The skin helps the fish maintain its balance of water and salts. If you hold a fish or damage its skin, you could kill it! The fish can actually leak or develop an infection.

shark skin denticles (magnification=250%)

Sharks, on the other hand, have very rough skin. It feels like sandpaper. That is because shark skin is made up of tiny, hard structures called **denticles** *(DEN-tick-uhlz).* Denticles are shaped like teeth, and they are made of the same materials as teeth, too (enamel, dentine, and pulp). These denticles all fit tightly together to form a tough armor. This shark armor helps the fish swim more quickly because it reduces the water's friction. The denticles on its skin are so prickly and sharp, they can injure small prey as the shark whips through the water. A handy way to snag lunch!

All about Gills

Fish have **gills** instead of lungs. Like our lungs, gills help fish get oxygen. But instead of getting oxygen from the air like we do, fish get oxygen from the water. Ocean water flows over a fish's gills, and oxygen is exchanged for carbon dioxide, which passes into the water.

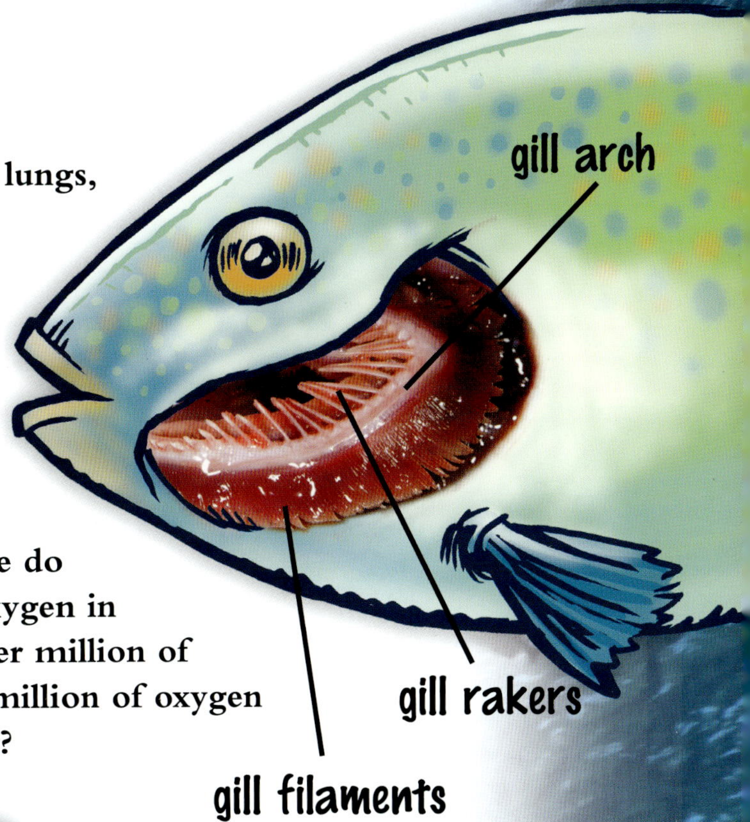

Scientists tell us that fish have a harder time breathing through their gills than we do through our lungs. There is a lot more oxygen in the air than in the water (200,000 parts per million of oxygen in the air versus 4 to 8 parts per million of oxygen in water). Aren't you glad you breathe air?

sea cucumber

giant octopus

Odd Organs

Each fall, the **sea cucumber** hides. Why? Because it is replacing its internal organs—literally. Its guts shrivel up and—presto!—two weeks later, it grows a new set. But if you pick up or disturb the sea cucumber in those two weeks, watch out! It will poop out all of its guts.

An **octopus** wins prizes in the heart department. The octopus has three hearts. Two hearts pump blood through its two gills. The third heart pumps blood through the body.

Sea Life Smarts

Highly evolved mammals with large brains, **dolphins** are believed to be the smartest creatures under the sea. The dolphin **brain** is actually larger than the human brain. It has two halves, just like the human brain, but it has four lobes instead of three. The fourth lobe deals with the senses—taste, touch, hearing, smell, and sight. Some think this fourth lobe allows dolphins to make complicated decisions.

The brain of the sperm whale weighs twenty pounds—the largest of any animal on earth.

Atlantic spotted dolphins

Cetaceans

Cetaceans *(suh-TAY-shunz)* (which include dolphins, whales, and porpoises) are curious, caring, sympathetic, playful, teasing, and spiteful. They enjoy playing tricks on one another. They communicate with each other by producing a huge variety of **sounds**—from the clicks of dolphins to the great groans of the **gray whales** to the strange and haunting songs of the **humpback whales.**

giant Pacific octopus

And remember Paul, the **octopus** at the Sea Life Aquarium in Oberhausen, Germany, that predicted the outcome of Germany's seven games in the 2010 FIFA World Cup soccer games, as well as the final? (Spain won against the Netherlands.) Whether or not Paul's predictions were a gimmick, the octopus is one smart **cephalopod.** The octopus may live for only two years, but scientists think it is as intelligent as the average house cat.

The **giant Pacific octopus** is not only smart, it is strong. Using its eight arms, it can move as much as 700 pounds.

At the National Zoo in Baltimore, the octopus is provided with a variety of simple objects—ranging from dog toys to snacks inside containers with lids—so it can explore new items that look, smell, or feel different. At the Monterey Bay Aquarium, handlers engage the two eleven-pound octopuses with games. To keep things interesting at feeding time, they present the octopuses with an orange ball or plastic maze. Handlers sometimes rearrange the tank, adding new rocks or fish, just as you might rearrange the furniture in your bedroom.

Facing or Fleeing Foes

LET'S FACE IT, THE SEA CONTAINS a world of animals, some (**predators**) that eat other animals, and some that are eaten (**prey**). Even predators can become prey. Whether they live in chilly arctic or warm tropical waters, fish have to protect themselves.

Chromatophores

Chromatophores are the pigments in fish skin that can expand and contract to change color.

sanddab

Camouflage

The **Pacific sanddab** spends its life on its side. After sweeping sand over its face, the sanddab changes color using its **chromatophores** *(kro-MAT-oh-forz)* to match its surroundings, similar to what a chameleon does. Gray-and-white rocky bottom? Gray-and-white sanddab.

An **Amazon leaf** fish is always in disguise. It looks like its name: a leaf. Larger fish do not bother it because the fish looks like a leaf floating in water.

Some **crabs** have their own way of hiding from predators. They blend into the seafloor by decorating their shells with sponges, barnacles, or algae.

A crab decorates its shell with sponge to disguise itself

pipefish

lionfish

leafy sea dragon

And try to find the **leafy sea dragon** among the seaweeds and sea grass where it lives.

Same with the **pipefish.** Speckled and red, the pipefish hides among the brightly colored coral. Just try to find it!

The **lionfish,** with its pattern of wild stripes, is easily disguised in the coral reefs of the Pacific and Indian oceans. It stalks its lunch—a small shrimp or crab—then snaps its jaws and swallows it whole. Gulp!

With their black-and-white stripes, **convict tang fish** may look like old-time prisoners, but the zebra stripes also confuse predators. Imagine thousands of black-and-white bodies scattering before you!

convict tang

cuttlefish

To disguise itself and communicate, the **Pharaoh cuttlefish** can change colors from metallic blue and green to gold and silver, and exhibit dots and stripes.

barreleye

Some fish are so see-through, it seems they have their own invisibility cloak. Check out the **barreleye.** This deep-water dweller has tubular eyes that you can see through its transparent head. This amazing fish was photographed using an underwater robot operated by the Monterey Bay Aquarium Research Institute.

The **big skate** scares away predators with the two large spots on its fins; predators think they are the eyes of a much bigger fish.

big skate

Lateral Lines

You know how you can sense when someone is standing near you? Fish can sense when other fish swim near them. Along each side of their sleek bodies, they have a row of scales known as a **lateral line.** These special sensory organs are filled with fluid and can help fish detect vibrations in the water. When a larger fish makes big ripples in the water, the littler fish knows it's time to boogie!

By detecting ripples in the water caused by struggling insects, **killfish** can close in on their prey. The lateral lines on **haddock** not only distinguish them from cod, but they may also help the fish to group together, or **shoal.** Blind **cavefish** have no eyes to help them find a meal, so they use their lateral lines to locate food in the water.

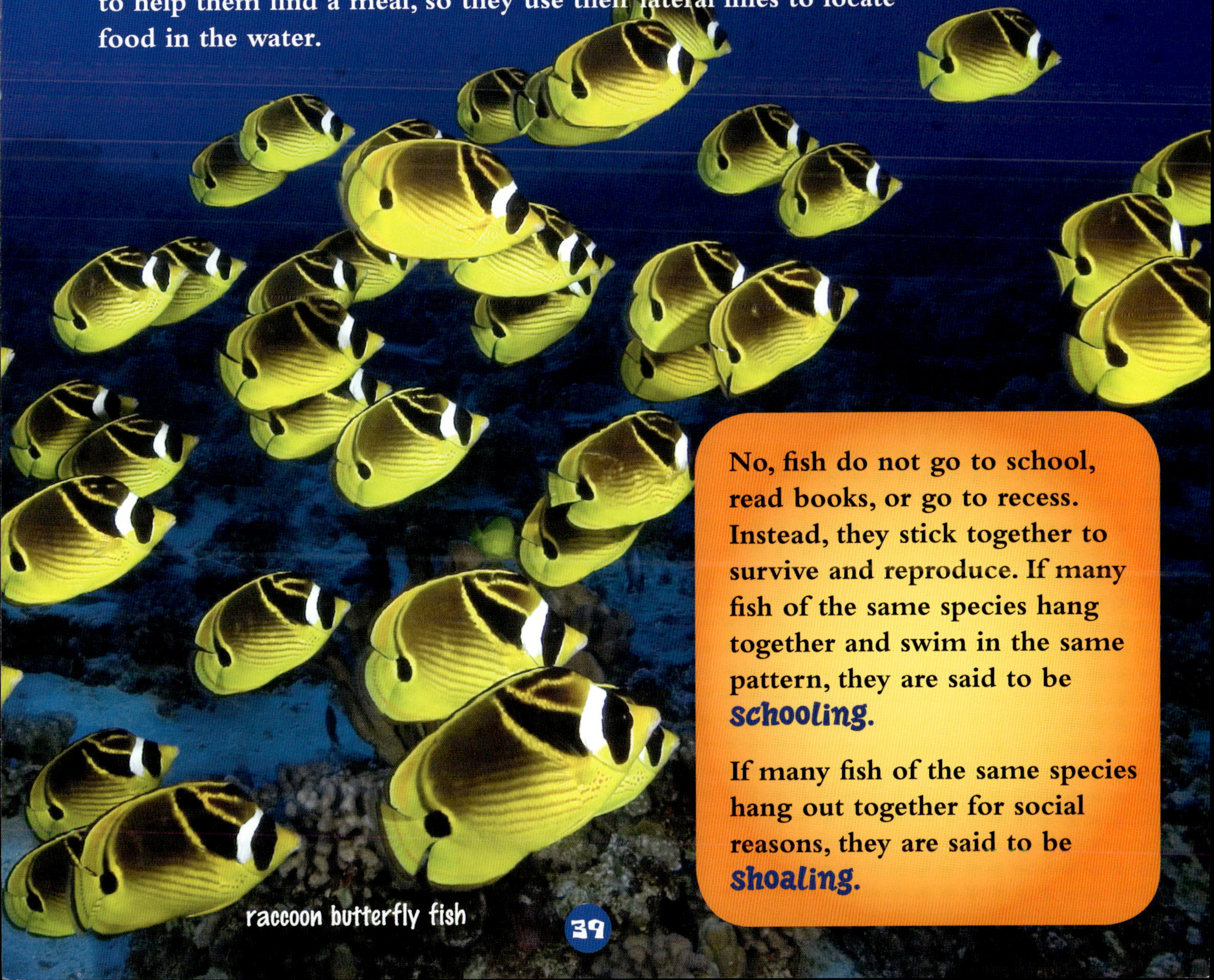

raccoon butterfly fish

No, fish do not go to school, read books, or go to recess. Instead, they stick together to survive and reproduce. If many fish of the same species hang together and swim in the same pattern, they are said to be **schooling.**

If many fish of the same species hang out together for social reasons, they are said to be **shoaling.**

The Poison Defense

For some fish—such as the **spotted ratfish** and the **rockfish**—the poison (or venom) is in their fins. For the **cabezon,** the poison is in their eggs, which is one way the fish protect the eggs from being eaten.

The most poisonous fish is the **death puffer,** or **maki-maki.** Just a tiny amount of this poison will kill a human, and there is no known antidote. Japanese eat maki-maki as a delicacy, but chefs practice for several years to learn to prepare it properly. Nearly fifty people die each year from poorly prepared maki-maki.

pufferfish

That's Shocking!

electric ray

Zzzzap! The **electric eel** can deliver a shock of nearly 650 volts. That's about five times the voltage in a wall socket in a house—enough to kill a human. But the eel's electricity isn't just about protection. Eels have poor vision, so they use their electrical receptors to help themselves get around. They can sense movements—even the heartbeats of other fish!

There are other species of freshwater "electric" fish as well. The **electric ray** or **torpedo fish** as well as the **freshwater electric catfish** and certain species of **stargazers** produce electricity from organs that are developed from modified muscle tissues. In addition to helping them navigate by using echolocation (see below), these fish produce electricity to kill their prey and scare away predators.

Dolphins use **echolocation** *(EHK-oh-lo-KAY-shun)* to communicate and to find food. Echolocation is animal sonar. By making a clicking sound and listening to its echo, whales and dolphins and eels can figure out the size, shape, distance, speed, and structure of an object. Whales also use it to figure out the lay of the land. By sending out signals, they can figure out what is around them: large schools of fish, large boats, rocks, or other landforms.

dolphins communicating by echolocation

You Help Me; I'll Help You

Several species help each other. Take **clownfish** and **anemones.** Clownfish escape from predators by hiding among the poisonous anemones. The fish is covered in a slimy mucus that protects it from the anemone's stinging tentacles. The clownfish also eats food scraps left over from the anemone's meals. In turn, the clownfish helps the anemone by defending it against predators and cleaning it of parasites. This is a **symbiotic relationship,** or one that benefits both animals.

Southern Stingrays

When **southern stingrays** need sprucing up, they visit **bluehead wrasses** and **Spanish hogfish.** These fish like to eat parasites and mucus from the stingray's body. **Señoritas** are also cleaner fish that eat parasites off larger fish.

Glow, Fish, Glow

The deep-sea **anglerfish** lives so far down in the ocean that it spends its whole life in the dark; it never sees the light of day. So this unusual fish creates its own light. On its nose, above its gaping mouth full of needlelike teeth, is a small fishing rod with a glowing "lure" at the end. Used only by female anglerfish, this luminous lure is a bit of flesh that is designed to draw prey close enough so that the angler can snatch a meal in its large jaws. The mighty anglerfish can eat a dinner twice its size by using its large jaws and flexible body.

Some fish, such as anglerfish, glow because of light-producing bacteria in their bodies. Others, such as deep-sea hatchet fish, produce light through a chemical reaction similar to a lightning bug.

Bioluminescence *(BY-oh-loo-mih-NESS-ents)* is a chemical process that creates light in ocean fish as well as in insects such as fireflies.

Hatchet fish have pale-blue lights on their bellies. These lights match the filtered sunlight seen from below, making hatchet fish hard to spot by predators swimming beneath them.

Slime, Burps, and, Yes, Gas

If you do some of the above, you may be asked to mind your manners! We may find these bodily functions rude, but they can be matters of survival for sea creatures.

Let's talk about slime. Although it makes us shiver, slime helps protect the skin of the **California moray eel,** which likes to hide in rock caves. And the **green moray eel** may look green under water, but it's actually covered with a brown mucus much like, well, you guessed it, the stuff in your nose.

To put itself to sleep, the **parrotfish** doesn't pull its covers up; it wraps itself in slime. Doesn't that sound cozy? Scientists think the slime hides the scent of the parrotfish and protects it from attack from predators, such as the moray eel.

archerfish squirting water to displace cricket

Archerfish

The **archerfish** is a water spitter. When it spots unwary prey—say an insect resting on a branch above the surface of the water—the archerfish can spit a jet of water to knock the bug off the plant and into the water. Now that's a good aim!

The spiraled shell of the **chambered nautilus** has spaces filled with gas that allow it to move up and down in the ocean. If it wants to dive, it simply adds liquid to its many chambers. Gas also helps the **Pharaoh cuttlefish** get around in the sea. The Pharaoh cuttlefish used to have an outer shell that evolved into an inner shell that is **porous** *(POR-us)*, which means liquids can leak through it. To move up and down in the water, the cuttlefish varies the amount of gas and liquid held in the shell's holes.

A **sand tiger shark** burps to adjust its ability to float. If it wants to hover in place—just like you do the dead man's float—it has to gulp and blow out air at the surface of the water.

Fish are marvelous creatures. Whether facing or fighting foes, changing colors to match their surroundings, carrying eggs in their mouths or lights on their heads, fish are funny, mysterious, and always fascinating.

chambered nautilus

Index

Credits

All illustrations by Robert Rath.

Photo credits:

Tom Stack/Tom Stack & Associates: pages 6-7 (parrotfish); page 8 (sea nettle jelly); page 16 (sea horse); page 17 (mermaid's purse); page 26 (peacock flounder); page 27 (hagfish); page 29 (Amazon River catfish); front cover and page 30 (butterfly fish); page 31 (gill, sea cucumber); page 36 (2 sanddabs); page 39 (snook); page 40 (rockfish)

David Fleetham/Tom Stack & Associates: front cover (angelfish); back cover (longfin spadefish); page 6 (clownfish); page 7 (fairy anthias, angelfish, blue jacks, circular batfish); page 8 (humpback whale, Atlantic bottlenose dolphin); page 16 (cuttlefish); page 18 (octopus with eggs); page 19 (bottlenose dolphin); page 20 (clownfish); page 25 (parrotfish); page 26 (hammerhead shark); page 28 (humpback whale); pages 32-33 (Atlantic spotted dolphins); page 36 (pipefish); page 37 (lionfish, leafy sea dragon); page 39 (raccoon butterfly fish); page 46 (chambered nautilus)

Andy Murch/Tom Stack & Associates: front cover and page 10 (whale shark); page 9 (giant cuttlefish, giant Pacific octopus); page 31 (giant octopus); page 33 (giant Pacific octopus); page 38 (big skate); page 40 (spotted ratfish)

Robert S. Michelson/Tom Stack & Associates: page 9 (northern lobster in eel grass); page 17 (Atlantic salmon eggs); page 21 (Atlantic salmon); page 29 (Atlantic wolf eel)

Terrence Ross/Tom Stack & Associates: front cover and page 17 (yellow-headed jawfish); page 20 (queen parrotfish, creole wrasse, shy hamlet); page 25 (spotted eagle ray); page 27 (barracuda); page 29 (queen parrotfish); page 36 (crab); page 38 (cuttlefish); page 41 (electric ray)

Scott Linstead/Tom Stack & Associates: page 45 (archerfish)

Jessica Solberg: page 8 (sea stars)

Bigstock Images: borders on pages 8-9, 16, 20, 25, 29, 30-31, 36-37, 38, 40-41, 44-45; page 24 (mola); page 27 (piranha); page 37 (convict tang); pages 42-43 (clownfish)

University of Cape Town: page 30 (denticles)

Monterey Bay Aquarium Research Institute: front cover and page 38 (barreleye)

About the Author

Caroline Patterson lives in Missoula, Montana, with her husband, son, and daughter. On top of writing children's books, she has published fiction in numerous literary anthologies and teaches poetry in the schools.